CDL Study Guide

★ 2022-2023 ★

Comprehensive Exam Prep Training Manual with All the Endorsements, Hazardous Materials and Topics Needed to Pass the Commercial Driver's License Exam at First Try.

By

MALCOLM WINDROW

Table of Contents

Introduction **9**

Chapter 1 What is CDL? **11**

1.1 Driver's License vs. CDL 13

1.2 Getting a CDL 16

1.3 Legal Aspects 18

1.4 Training 22

Chapter 2 How to apply for a Commercial Driving license? **25**

2.1 Eligibility Criteria for Obtaining a Commercial Driver's License (CDL) 26

2.2 Steps to Obtain a Commercial Driver's License in 2022 27

2.3 Steps to get Class A License 33

2.4 Steps to get Class B License 35

2.5 Steps to get Class C License 37

Chapter 3 Types of CDL **39**

3.1 Class A CDL 41

3.2 Class B CDL 43

3.3 Class C CDL 45

3.4 Class A Or B: Manual Vs. Automatic 47

Chapter 4 Commercial Driving License Jobs 49

4.1 Driver of a long-distance cargo truck 50

4.2 Bus Driver 51

4.3 Transportation of Heavy Equipment 51

4.4 Dispatcher 51

4.5 Truck driving Instructor 53

4.6 Bus Driver 53

4.7 Operator/Owner 54

4.8 Terminal Manager 55

4.9 Driver of a local truck 55

Chapter 5 Overseas CDL 57

5.1 CDL In the United States 58

5.2 CDL In the United Kingdom 62

5.3 CDL In Australia 64

5.4: CDL In New Zealand 66

5.5: CDL In Hong Kong 68

5.6: Is Overseas Trucking and CDL The Right Career Path for You? 69

5.7: You Are Attentive in Learning About Other Cultures 70

5.8: You Are Not Intimidated by The Prospect of Higher Criteria 70

5.9: You Are Fluent in Another Language 71

Chapter 6 Requirements for CDL 75

6.1 Training Requirements 80

6.2 Health and Physical Requirements 84

6.3 Written and Knowledge-Based Examinations 90

Chapter 7 Endorsements 93

7.1 (H) Hazardous Substances and Materials (HAZMAT) 94

7.2 (N) Tank Transport Vehicle 95

7.3 (P) Transportation of Passengers 95

7.4 (S) Bus Transportation Services 96

7.5 (X) Tank and Dangerous Materials Transport 97

7.6 T-Signal Endorsement 98

7.7 CDL Restrictions 98

7.8 Restriction on E 99

7.9 Restriction (F) 100

7.10 Restriction (G) 100

7.11 Restriction on K's 101

7.12 L Restriction Is a Restriction That Applies to A Person ... 101

7.13 Restriction on The Use M 102

7.14 N Restriction 103

7.15 O Restriction 103

7.16 V Restriction 104

7.17 Restriction X 105

7.18 Restriction on the Z 105

7.19 Restriction (B) 105

7.20 Restriction on P 105

Conclusion.. 109

Introduction

Suppose you want to drive big, heavy, or unwanted and repeated hazardous material trucks for business reasons in the United States. In that case, you'll need a commercial driver's license (often known as a CDL). Several kinds of commercial motorized vehicles (CMVs) need the possession of a valid commercial driver's license (CDL). Obtaining one or more specific endorsements, including such Air Brakes, Dangerous Chemicals (Hazmat), Tankers, and Passenger Cars, may also be necessary to operate a vehicle regarding the air brakes, a vehicle with a tank, a truck transporting hazardous substances, or a passenger vehicle, respectively.

A commercial driver's license (CDL) enables a client to operate a business motor vehicle on public highways. Regulations governing the operation of motorized vehicles are enforced by the Massachusetts Registrar of Motor Vehicles and the United States Department of Transportation. Learn how to get, renew, or renew your commercial driver's license and other valuable information.

A written exam is required for each CDL and endorsement; some also need to pass a skills test and the written test. Certain kinds of endorsements have extra conditions that must be met. The driver must also be fingerprinted and submit to a security threat assessment by the Transportation Security Administration (TSA) to transport hazardous materials.

For those wishing to earn a Class A or B CDL, one must first complete theory training from an authorized theory training provider registered on the FMCSA Accredited Training Registry, which may be found here (TPR). Your training records will be sent to the TPR by your provider after you have completed the training course. After that, your State's Department of Motor Vehicles (DMV) will allow us to take the formal document knowledge exam for a CLP. Furthermore, you must undergo behind-the-wheel (BTW) instruction from a BTW training provider who has been authorized by TPR and is listed in the TPR. Your training records will be sent to the TPR by your provider after you have completed the training course. After that, your State's Department of Motor Vehicles (DMV) will let you take your official CDL skills exam.

Chapter 1

What is CDL?

You never understand how and when you might be hit by a car when you are behind the wheel of a motor vehicle. It requires you to have cost-effective driving skills, but it also necessitates a good sharp mind because you never understand how and when you might have been involved in a collision. The Police Act, 1988 makes it obligatory for every vehicle owner to possess a valid driving license to maintain their driving under regulatory control and be legally permitted to operate their car on Indigenous highways and byways.

A commercial driver's license is required for those who operate a commercial vehicle for business reasons, which most commercial vehicle drivers are. We all know that commercial vehicles, including light and heavy vehicles, are primarily used to transport goods or transport passengers. It is necessary to get a driver's license to ensure that a man has excellent driving abilities and is familiar with various automobiles since he will be behind the vehicle's wheel. This assurance is given in a commercial driving license, which functions similarly to a permanent driving license.

When driving a commercial car or running a company involving one, a person may encounter challenges distinct from those encountered by someone who owns and operates a private vehicle. Furthermore, because commercial vehicles are always driven on highways, drivers must be more alert and aware of various traffic rules to avoid accidents.

A commercial driving license, also known as a commercial driver's license, is a government-issued document that certifies that the holder is authorized to operate motor vehicles intended to transport goods and people on public roads and public transportation systems in Indigenous cities other public areas.

The acquisition of a commercial driving license is required for anyone wishing to join the transportation sector, which includes the business of operating/driving trucks, vehicles, and buses on Indigenous highways. These licenses are issued by the regional transport office and require the motorist to pass a series of academic and driving examinations before being awarded the license in question. After obtaining a regular driving license, it is possible to earn a commercial driving license. A commercial driving license is identical to a regular driving license in that it may only be used to drive commercial vehicles.

1.1 Driver's License vs. CDL

It is a legal authorization (or the official document proving such authorization) for a person to function one or more types of motorized cars (such as motorbikes, automobiles, trucks, or buses) on a public road, and it is issued to that individual by the state. Such licenses are often made of plastic and are equivalent to a credit or debit card. The term "driving permit" is used in most international accords, like the Vienna Convention of Road Traffic, adopted in 1961. The local spelling variation is used in the portions of this page that are peculiar to each nation.

The regulations governing the licensing of drivers differ from one country to the next. In some countries, a permit is only provided after the receiver has completed a driving test, while in others, a permit must be obtained before the recipient is allowed to begin driving. Permits for motor vehicles, notably heavy trucks, and passenger cars, are often issued under several classifications. The complexity of the driver's test varies significantly across countries, as do criteria such as age, the needed degree of competence, and the amount of driving practice required to pass.

An official "Genehmigung" (permission) first from Grand Ducal administration to drive his Motorwagen on public highways was issued to Karl Benz, the creator of the modern automobile, in 1888 after neighbors complained about the smell and odor of his vehicle. Until the beginning of the twentieth century, European authorities provided comparable licenses to drive motor vehicles on an as-needed basis if they issued them.

Mandatory licensing for motorists inside the United Kingdom became effective on January 1, 1904, and after the passage of the Motor Car Law 1903, which King George V. Upon request signed, every automobile owner was required to register the vehicle to their local government body and be able to provide documentation proving that their vehicle was registered.

The qualifying examination age was established at seventeen years old. When the "driving license" was issued, its possessor had "freedom of the road," with a maximum speed restriction.

With the passage of the Motor Vehicle Act in 1934, the practice of mandatory testing was established. Anyone who operates a motorized vehicle on public roads must have a valid driver's license under the law. A driver's license will indicate that you are physically healthy and can operate a car in a certain class. What is the variation between such a commercial or non-commercial license for driver's licenses?

Individuals with a commercial driver's license will be permitted to drive commercial cars, vehicles used for business reasons. Individuals with a non-commercial driver's license, on the other hand, will only be capable of driving private automobiles, with a few exemptions.

A commercial driver's license permits you to operate various vehicles with a few restrictions. Depending on the CDL license, a commercial driver's license may be upgraded to include an endorsement of 15 people or more. The legislation governing business driver's licenses is quite precise. As a result, you may only apply in the state you are now residing in. You must be above the age of 21 to apply for hazardous goods transportation. Your CDL must also show that you have a valid endorsement for hazardous materials transportation.

Driver's licenses for non-commercial vehicles are limited to those that weigh no more than 8000 pounds. In certain jurisdictions, teenagers as early as 15 may receive a learner's permit for operating a passenger car. A non-commercial driver's license (non-CDL) will enable you to operate passenger cars, trucks, vans, and sport utility vehicles. When driving with a learner's permit, you must be accompanied by a licensed driver over 21 when the operator is under 21.

Your driver's license will be validated with any requirements that the driver has, such as driving with a class and when you are permitted to operate a vehicle throughout the day. The same is true when obtaining a motorbike license.

1.2 Getting a CDL

You obligation be at minimum eighteen years old to get a driver's license. Is there anything specific you need to learn? No, you do not. However, it is recommended that you seek training with a driving test to provide you with the information and skills necessary to become the greatest CDL driver possible. Obtaining a commercial driver's license takes an average of one week. It will take longer to master the fundamentals of driving if you attend a commercial driving school; on average, it will take 4 to 6 weeks. Some states demand that you must attend a commercial driver's school before they would get you into a commercial driver's license, while others do not (CDL).

We recommend that all commercial drivers join a commercial driving course to develop their skills, check all the boxes, and lower the risk factor because you will be operating in either your employer's or your cars. Keeping your driving as safe as possible and avoiding accidents will be your primary concerns. For someone to operate a vehicle flawlessly and with extreme caution requires years of training and expertise. During your time at the school, you will understand safe driving techniques and how to take care of your cargo and other drivers on the road. Driving a truck is never tough; only the aspects of the roadway provide a challenge to drivers. We strongly advise all commercial drivers to familiarize themselves with their state's commercial driver's license manual. It is accessible at the Department of Transportation in most states and may be obtained by calling the State's DMV (DMV). You may go to the Transport department Vehicles' official website. Everything in the guide will be used as a basis for your exam.

1.3 Legal Aspects

Commercial driver's licenses (CDLs) have been necessary to operate specific commercial automobiles (CMVs) from the first day of April 1992. The sorts of vehicles and activities that need a CDL are listed below. To ensure the safety of commercial drivers, the FMCSA had created and released guidelines for state exams and licensing of commercial drivers. Specifically, these rules ensure states only issue CDLs to such commercial motor vehicle drivers after the driver has passed knowledge and skills exams performed by the state and applicable to the kind of vehicle that driver plans to operate, among other requirements.

Drivers who engage in interstate, regional, or international commerce who drive a car that fulfills one or more classes of a commercial motor vehicle (CMV) must get and maintain a CDL. When a CDL holder performs the abilities exam in a vehicle that does not include key equipment found in certain commercial motor vehicles, restrictions are put on the CDL. The following are some examples of these constraints in action. As a result, drivers should undertake the skills exam in the same kind of vehicle for pursuing a CDL to avoid any limitations.

Individual state laws set the age limit for obtaining a CDL. The minimum for obtaining a CDL in all states, such as the Columbia, is 18 years old, apart from Hawaii, where the minimum age is 21 years old. According to the Federal Motorized Carrier Safety Administration, commercial vehicle drivers must be 21 years old or older to operate a commercial vehicle within interstate commerce. Although 49 states let 18 through 20-year-olds get a commercial driver's license, they are only permitted to operate a commercial vehicle inside the state where the CDL was obtained, i.e., in intrastate trade. Drivers who carry hazardous items and need placards must be 21 years old or older to be eligible to do so. Additional age restrictions differ from State to State.

After being signed into law on November 15, 2021, the Infrastructure Investment, as well as Jobs Act, includes an amendment establishing a three-year apprenticeship program that would allow 18- to 20-year-old with such a CDL to continue operating in interstate commerce after completing supervised learning with an older and more experienced driver before being allowed to drive in multiple states.

When driving commercial automobiles (CMVs), mostly tractor-trailers, before 1992, sophisticated skills and knowledge were necessary that were in addition to and above those required when driving a car or other light vehicle. Large vehicle and bus drivers were required to get a commercial driver's license (CDL) before establishing the CDL in 1992, and licensing criteria varied from State to State. Due to this lack of training, many avoidable road fatalities and accidents have occurred.

When the Act was passed in 1992, all drivers who operated a commercial motorized vehicle were required to own a CDL. The FHWA has created guidelines for evaluating drivers who want to get a driver's license. States in the United States are only permitted to issue CDLs after a written test exam has been administered either by the state or an authorized testing center. A commercial driver's license (CDL) is required if the vehicle fulfills one of the commercial motors (CMV) requirements stated above.

In addition, certain states may demand a CDL to operate some other types of vehicles. For example, any driver licensed in New Jersey who drives a bus, limousine, and van used for employment and intended to carry 8 to 15 people must have a commercial driver's license lawfully carry passengers in city buses and other vehicles mentioned in article 19-A of the State's Motor and Traffic Law, a driver's license in New York should be held by a commercial driver's license. Drivers licensed in California must hold a commercial driver's license (CDL) if their principal work involves driving, regardless of operating a commercial vehicle. A commercial vehicle carries persons or goods for hire regularly in California. Additionally, in California, having a commercial driver's license lowers the threshold for receiving a Driving Under Influence ticket from 0.08 percent to 0.04 percent blood alcohol level.

Prospective licensees should check their State's CDL requirements by consulting the State's CDL Manual. Most states demand that you have a driver's license (for automobiles) before you may get a Commercial Driver's License.

1.4 Training

The educational requirements differ from State to State. Depending on the state (such as Ohio), you may be required to complete 160 hours of classroom and on-the-road training. Training may be achieved by finishing a valid CDL training program via a truck driving school that the DMV has authorized. Truck driver training programs are specifically designed to provide potential truck drivers with the skills and knowledge to operate a truck properly and safely. Topics covered include map reading, route planning, conformance with United States Department of Transportation regulations, backing up, turning, trying to hook a trailer, and highway driving.

This kind of training is designed to assist future truck drivers in passing the CDL skills and knowledge examinations and driver training tactics such as skid prevention and recovery and other emergency measures for circumstances such as a runaway trailer hydroplaning. A conventional non-commercial driver's education course, like the driver's education class offered in a high school, does not give these programs' level of training. Several certified CDL training schools are located around the United States, and several trucking corporations run their training facilities.

Is there anything specific you need to learn? No, you do not. However, it is recommended that you seek training with a driving instructor to provide you with the information and skills necessary to become the greatest CDL driver possible. Obtaining a commercial driver's license takes an average of one week. It will take longer to master the fundamentals of driving if you attend a commercial driving school; on average, it will take 4 to 6 weeks. Some states demand that you must attend a commercial driver's school before they would provide you with a business driver's license, while others do not (CDL).

We recommend that all commercial drivers attend a commercial driver's ed to develop their skills, check all the boxes, and lower the risk factor since you will be driving in either your employer's or your cars. Keeping your driving as safe as possible and avoiding accidents will be your primary concerns. For someone to operate a vehicle flawlessly and with extreme caution requires years of training and expertise. During your time at the school, you will understand safe driving techniques and how to take care of your cargo and other drivers on the road. Driving a truck is never tough; only the aspects of the roadway provide a challenge to drivers.

We strongly advise all commercial drivers to familiarize themselves with their state's commercial driver's license manual. It is accessible at the Department of Transportation in most states and may be obtained by calling the State's DMV (DMV). You may go to the Transport department Vehicles' official website. Everything in the guide will be used as a basis for your exam.

Chapter 2

How to apply for a Commercial Driving license?

According to the Motor Vehicle Act of 1988, the government issues a commercial driving vehicle license to drivers who demonstrate that they are qualified to operate a commercial vehicle on public roads. It is equivalent to a personal driving license, with the added benefit of being able to use it for both business and personal cars.

Commercial vehicles, including trucks, automobiles, buses, and other similar vehicles, transport people and commodities on highways and roads. Driving a commercial vehicle/automotive without a CDL is a criminal offense.

Compared to driving a non-commercial vehicle, operating the commercial motor vehicle (CMV) necessitates a higher degree of education, experience, skills, & physical capabilities. An applicant for a Commercial Driver's License (CDL) must pass knowledge and skills tests tailored to these higher criteria to be granted the license.

Additionally, while driving any motor vehicle on public roadways, CDL holders are held to higher standards than non-licensed drivers. Serious traffic offenses committed by the CDL holder might hurt their ability to keep their CDL certification active and active.

2.1 Eligibility Criteria for Obtaining a Commercial Driver's License (CDL)

To be eligible to apply for just a commercial driving license, you must satisfy the requirements listed below:

- You are above 18 to be eligible for a commercial driver's license.
- The educational requirement should be a passing grade in the eighth grade or above.
- Should have a learners' permit.

- To be eligible/qualified for a commercial driver's license, you must complete instruction at a government-sponsored vehicle training school or just one linked with the government.

Obtaining a Commercial Driver's License (CDL)

The fundamental criteria for all licensing classes (A, B, & C) are the same. There are, however, additional criteria for each license class, which are detailed in their corresponding parts of this document.

2.2 Steps to Obtain a Commercial Driver's License in 2022

1. You must be at least 20-21 years old (at least 18-19 years of age drive intrastate)
2. Driver instruction from FMCSA-approved training institutions is required if you want to earn a Class A or Class B commercial driver's license (CDL) in any state.
3. Submit the CDL Application for your state, along with the proper fee.
4. Please provide identification and Social Security number confirmation (see your state's rules for further information).

5. Provide evidence of state and federal residence in the United States.
6. Both duly filled, return the Medical Examination Report Form and the Medical Examiner's Certificate Form.
7. Pass a vision examination
8. Pass a knowledge-based test
9. After leaving/passing the exam, you will receive a Commercial Learner's Permit (CLP)
10. Before scheduling the CDL road skills assessment, you must wait at least 14 days. Pass the pre-trip inspection with flying colors
11. Pass the road skills & driving test with flying colors (must bring own vehicle)
12. Obtaining your new CDL after passing the exam (you may also submit a 10-Year Record Check if you formerly held a driver's license in a state or jurisdiction later than one where you have been applying for CDL) and then paying the required fees.

If you want to earn a Class A / Class B CDL, you must first complete theory instruction from an authorized theory training organization listed on the FMCSA's Training Directory (TPR). Your training records will be sent to the TPR by your provider after you have completed the training course. After that, your state's Department of Motor Vehicles (DMV) will certainly take the formal document knowledge exam for a CLP. Furthermore, it would help if you underwent behind-the-wheel (BTW) instruction from a BTW training provider who has been authorized by TPR and is listed in the TPR. Your training records will be sent to the TPR by your provider after you have completed the training course. After that, your state's Department of Motor Vehicles (DMV) will let you complete the official CDL skills exam.

It is important to note that unless you're a military veteran who has prior experience trying to drive military buses as well as military trucks, the state could waive any or all the succeeding written tests: CDL General Understanding, Passenger, Tanker, as well as Hazmat, if you can provide proof of pertinent military experience. In addition, every state will enable you to forego taking the driving exam.

Obtaining your commercial driver's license allows you to become a member of an industry that is vital to the functioning of the United States economy. While everyone is aware that trucks are on the road, most are unaware that those trucks are responsible for carrying 70% of all freight inside the United

States - freight worth over $670 billion, which is more than the whole nation of Switzerland's annual GDP!

The federal government imposes the fundamental standards for the different kinds of commercial driver's licenses, but states are free to impose extra restrictions that they see appropriate.

According to federal law, if you want to drive commercially over state lines, you must be 21 years old or older. Many states, however, will only give a CDL for intrastate driving to persons who are 18 years old or older; consult your state's requirements for more information. The following documents will be required once you apply for your commercial driver's license and have completed the CDL application form for your state: your social security number, proof of identification, and evidence of residence in the state where you want to work.

In most states, your social security card, a Medicare ID card, a current ID card from any branch of the US Armed Forces (retired, active, reserve, or dependent), or a military separation record, also known as a DD-214, are all acceptable forms of identification to prove your social security number. Check with your state to see whether they accept any other kinds of identification as verification of your social security number. The list of papers that may be used to prove your identification varies even more from state to state. For example, a valid US birth certificate, as well as certified copy of a valid US birth certificate, a valid US passport, a valid USCIS American Indian Card, a valid military ID card, a certificate either of Citizenship as well as Naturalization, a Permanent Resident Card, or a Temporary Resident ID Card, are all acceptable forms of identification. Probably, your state recognizes a variety of additional papers as identification, so it's advisable to consult your state's CDL handbook or DMV website for the most up-to-date information.

State-specific criteria for proof of residence will be different as well. According to some states, such as Alabama, you may only be required to submit a single utility bill copy; whereas others, such as California, may require you to submit two or three documents from a list of close to eighteen various possibilities, all of which must have the same posting speech as the address listed on your CDL application. Remember to check your state's DMV website to ensure that you won't encounter any difficulties. You must also require/provide evidence that you are medically able to drive professionally. It is in addition to supplying documentation of your forename, birth date, place of residence, age, & social security number. A vision test, which you will do in connection with the implementation of your CDL examinations, will be the most straightforward part of this procedure; nevertheless, the more involved aspect will need you to provide appropriate medical records.

The new legislation/lawmaking will require you to submit two documents to your state commercial driver's licensing agency beginning in 2022, regardless of whether you are driving intrastate or interstate: the Medical Examinations Report Forms (MCSA-5875) and the Medical Examiner's Certificate Form (MCSA-5876). Suppose you want to drive over state lines. In that case, you must have your medical documents filled out by a medical examiner who is certified by the National Registration System of Certified Medical Examiners. If these documents are necessary for your work duties, your employer is responsible for covering their cost.

After submitting all the appropriate documentation, you must pass the required exams. All commercial driver's licenses applicants must pass an eyesight examination and a knowledge examination.

You will be issued a commercial learner's permit once passed these tests (CLP). According to the Federal regulations, you should have the CLP for a minimal level of 14 days until you can sit for the road skills test. A CLP may be valid for one year & nonrenewable, or it may be valid for much less than a year and renewable, depending on the state that issued it. It is important to note that the potential employer may include special restrictions just on job applications to attract CDL drivers with the highest levels of qualifications.

2.3 Steps to get Class A License

To obtain a Class A Driver's License, everything is necessary to get standard CDL drivers who have completed driver education from FMCSA-approved training institutions to pass the regular CDL knowledge exam and the knowledge test for Combination Vehicles.

Bring a class A vehicle to the highway/road skills exam and fill out an application for the needed class A certifications. Class A certification/license is mandatory when driving a mixture of vehicles/ Automotives with a combined weight of more than 27,000 pounds, and indeed the automotive being dragged weighs more than 15,000 pounds, as described above. Commercial vehicles with trailers and semi-trailers with three or more axles would be included in many jurisdictions.

The Class, a Commercial Driver's License, is the complete commercial driver's license that may be obtained. A truck with double & triple trailers and several other commercial motor vehicles are permitted to be operated under your supervision by top trucking firms. To get a Class A license/permit, you must complete all the requirements previously outlined and pass a Combination written exam. First and foremost, you must bring a class A car to your driving skills evaluation. Depending on your specific vehicle and the sort of career you are pursuing, you may be required to take additional endorsement examinations, like the Double Triple endorsement exam, which will enable you to tow double or triple trailers and other tests.

The pneumatic brakes test will also be required if your vehicle is equipped with these devices. As soon as you have completed all the appropriate paperwork, submitted all required documents, and passed your written and driving exams, you will get your novel class A commercial driver's license!

2.4 Steps to get Class B License

Everything you need to obtain a standard CDL is in place: you must complete driving lessons from FMCSA-approved training institutions, pass the general CDL proficiency test, carry a class B vehicle to the road skills test, and apply for any requisite class B endorsement deals before taking your road skills test (air brakes, tanks, etc.) A Class B license is required if you plan to drive any single vehicle that weighs more than 26,000 pounds & the GVWR (gross vehicle weight rating) of any vehicle being towed is less than 10,000 pounds. A class B license is sufficient for transporting most of the weight since most single vehicle carries the weight. You do not need either a double endorsement or the combination endorsement. However, if your vehicle is equipped with air brakes or you want to tow a trailer, you must obtain endorsements for those features. In most states, you'll need an air brake endorsement if you want to operate a trash truck. The secret to receiving the new class B license and going on the road is simply checking off the boxes: finish the paperwork, submit your medical documentation, pass all your examinations with flying colors, pay your costs, and do you.

2.5 Steps to get Class C License

To get a Class C License, you must first complete the CDL application process, pass the general CDL knowledge exam, bring a class C vehicle to the road skills test, and apply for the appropriate certifications (Hazmat, passenger, and school bus, etc.) To operate a vehicle that transfers more than 16 people or hazardous products, you must have a class C driver's license. Class C licenses are obtained like class A or class B licenses, except that the kind of vehicle you would be driving will determine the procedure to follow. The only thing that distinguishes the class C license from other types of licenses is that you should apply for specific endorsements to use it. A passenger transport endorsement will be required if your business is only focused on providing passenger transportation. Driving a school bus necessitates having the driver's certification and the passenger endorsement on your license. The school bus endorsement necessitates the ability to load and unload students and operate stop signs, lights, and other equipment on the bus. You'll need the Hazmat endorsement if you're carrying hazardous products. In the case of hazardous chemicals, you will additionally be required to submit to extra state or TSA background checks before working with them. Additional safety tests for school bus drivers may be required by your state, which should be available on the state DMV website. Any needed is that you complete and submit your paperwork and all medical papers, take & pass all relevant exams, pay all applicable fees, and then go through whatever security checks before promptly receiving your fresh CDL class C license.

Chapter 3

Types of CDL

Rendering to the Bureau of Labor Statistics, transportation and the moving of products have been among the fastest increasing segments of the labor sector among small enterprises. Indeed's job-hunting website reports that growth among professional drivers has increased by 190 percent over the past three years, outpacing growth in every other small company sector, including building and healthcare.

If you are trying to employ drivers for your local company or if you are aspiring to be a driver, you should be aware that certain vehicle operators require specialty commercial driver's licenses

(CDLs) as well as special certifications regardless of the type of vehicle to be driven, the material or people to be transported, and the location of the vehicle. Drivers from certain commercial cars must obtain a professional driver's license under federal regulations. To operate commercial motor vehicles (CMVs), such as farm equipment, semi-trucks, garbage trucks, and passenger buses, you must have a Commercial Driver's License. If you want to work on the road or in a workplace, you'll require a commercial driver's license (CDL). It is determined by the type of CDL you hold that the types of vehicles you are licensed to drive are classified as follows: Classes A, B, And class C. The gross vehicle rating (GVWR) of the vehicle and other special regulations are also considered in CDL categorization. To operate a professional motor vehicle, one must have extremely specialized knowledge and skills. Before 1986, however, several states let anybody with an automobile driver's license operate a commercial motor vehicle. As a result, numerous drivers were operating commercial motor vehicles (CMVs) without sufficient training.

The Industrial Motor Vehicle Safety Law was signed on October 27, 1986, by President Ronald Reagan. This law made it essential for all commercial vehicle drivers to possess a license (CDL). In addition to guaranteeing that delivery drivers and heavy truck operators receive extensive training and certification, this law has increased highway safety. On February 7, 2022, the Department of Transportation (DOT) announced a further improvement to driver training standards. Candidates seeking a Class A or Class B commercial driver's license, or an H, P, or S endorsement, will be required to complete instruction from FMCSA-approved training institutes listed in the FMCSA's Training Registry as of that date if they wish to be considered for a CDL or an H, P, or S tacit approval (TPR). Is it even necessary to get a CDL license? Which is better: a Class A or a Class B commercial driver's license if you do? You've pondered driving without a particular license, in which case you'll want to hire a CDL ticket attorney to represent you. Licenses for commercial drivers are required by law for anyone who operates a vehicle or a combo of a vehicle and a trailer that weighs more than 26,001 pounds.

On the other hand, Separate classes specify the types of vehicles that a licensee is capable of driving and operating. What are the classes, and which license do you require are the next questions? So, here we explain each type thoroughly.

3.1 Class A CDL

A Class A CDL certification typically opens the most doors for a driver regarding work options. The Federal Motor Carrier Affiliation defines CDL A trucks as "any combination of vehicles with a gross combination addition to taking into account or gross pairing weight of 11,794 kilograms or more (26,001 lbs. or more), whichever is larger, inclusive of a towed unit(s) with such a gross vehicle rating or gross vehicle mass of more than 4,536 kilograms (10,000 pounds), whichever is greater." Once you have obtained your CDL A license, you can apply for further endorsements that will allow you to operate a wider range of special vehicles. These endorsements necessitate further written and, in some cases, skills testing to be granted the endorsement. It is advisable to acquire the right license for your vehicle or weight class to avoid any need for careless driving attorneys. Class A license enables the licensee to operate any mixture of vehicles with a total vehicle weight ranking of 26,001 pounds or higher. In addition, pulling other vehicles weighing 10,000 pounds or more is included in this weight category. Moreover, a Category A CDL driver who has received the necessary endorsements can operate various commercial vehicles.

1. Tractor-trailers
2. Livestock transport vehicles
3. Combinations of trucks and trailers
4. Double and triple trailers, flatbeds, semi-trailers

Additionally, with this category, a driver could also operate Class B or C vehicles, provided with the appropriate endorsements. Therefore, Class A licenses are reserved for some of the largest and most complicated cars on the road today. You may also be eligible to drive some Class B or Class C cars with such a Class A CDL, depending on the endorsements you have. Vehicles such as livestock carriers, tractor-trailers, and passenger vans are examples of vehicles you can drive with a Class A license. If you intend to succeed as a professional under trucker, a class A commercial driver's license is ideal.

3.2 Class B CDL

When examining which vehicles require a commercial driver's license, you're likely to discover that a Class B CDL license is one of the most versatile options available for most common commercial transportation needs. This license applies to single cars with an overall mass of up to renewable - energy pounds. This license is valid for one vehicle only. Additionally, it permits the towing of that other vehicle weighing no and over 10,000 pounds. While this may be a substantial limitation, a Class B driver can operate a wide variety of commercial vehicles with the right endorsements. It is necessary to acquire this license to operate any single vehicle that is not attached to a container (commercial vehicles that have a linked cab and cargo place that has combined weight and is more than 26 thousand pounds while the trucks usually weigh less than 10 thousand pounds. The following vehicles are used: straight trucks, large coaches (such as city buses), segment buses, box trucks (such as delivery vehicles and furniture delivery vehicles), and dump trucks on small trailers. Some Class C automobiles with the appropriate endorsements are available. The passenger transport sector or the manufacture of goods and materials are two industries that commercial vehicle drivers with B And class commercial licenses can support with their vehicles.

Passenger endorsement on a CDL-B is required for drivers in the hospitality business who transport passengers to and from hotels and airports. They are also required to run rental car shuttle and regular bus, public bus, tour bus, urban transport, and other services. Depending just on the nature of the business, vehicle operators may be required to travel locally, nationally, and between metropolitan areas.

A CDL-B driver who does not have a "P" - Passengers approval on their license may operate large straight vehicles (weighing more than 26,000 lbs.), such as dump trucks and non-trailer box vans, but cannot transport passengers. Commercial driver's license (CDL) holders complete pre-trip vehicle checks, report safety or equipment problems to the dispatch, and must comply with United States Department of Transportation rules and regulations, such as the accurate updating of all logs and records. Straight trucks, box trucks, delivery trucks, couriers, and dump trucks are all examples of commercial vehicles.

A Class B CDL is like a Category A CDL in that it allows a legal chauffeur to operate vehicles that are classified at a lower level of classification. Therefore, a Class B driver can drive Class C vehicles if they have received the required endorsements.

3.3 Class C CDL

Class C commercial driver's license is a categorization for various smaller transport automobiles. For instance, if a driver transports at least 16 people, including themselves, they must have a Class C license. In addition, this categorization is required for the carriage of hazardous materials on public transit. As a result, if you plan to own and operate a HAZMAT vehicle, a passenger van, or a pickup truck carrying a trailer, you may be required to obtain this license.

Required while operating a single vehicle with a gross vehicle weight rating (GVWR) of least 26,001 pounds, when towing another automobile with a gross vehicle weight rating of less than £ 10, or when transporting 16 or more people, including the driver.

Double/triple trailers, buses, oil tankers, and hazardous materials vehicles are available. Owners of Class C licenses are permitted to operate specific types of cars. According to the Transport department Vehicles' website, drivers who hold a Class C license are permitted to operate the following vehicles:

1. 2-axle car with a rated rating (GVWR) of less than 26,000 pounds
2. A 3-axle vehicle with such a gross vehicle rating (GVWR) of less than 6,001 pounds
3. House car with a length of 40 feet or less
4. Three-wheel motorcycle with two wheels in the front or back
5. A vanpool vehicle designed to transport more than ten people, but no more than fifteen people, including the driver.

According to the DMV website, drivers with Class C licenses can tow a single car with a total vehicle load rating (GVWR) of less than 10,000 pounds. The towing of a trailer bus or 5th travel trailer weighs less than 10,000 lbs.

A fifth-wheel truck with a gross vehicle weight rating (GVWR) ranging between 10,000 to 15,000 lbs. is also permitted. If you are a farmer or work for a farmer, a Class C license will allow you to take a vehicle with a total vehicle weight rating (GVWR) of less than 26,0001 lbs. if used for farm-related reasons.

3.4 Class A Or B: Manual Vs. Automatic

When planning to obtain a Class A or B CDL, keep in mind the transmission you will be training with and the transmission you will be applying for. For instance, if you are practicing with your CLP in an automatic vehicle and discover that the CDL driver's test requires you to paddle-shift transmission, you will most likely not have the abilities necessary to pass the test. Research the industries and positions you are interested in applying for to comprehend the types of car transmissions employed in those industries or occupations. If you acquire an automatic CDL, a marking will be placed on your license, indicating that you have only been taught on automated vehicles. It may make it more difficult for you to obtain employment in an industry where manual cars are used.

Chapter 4

Commercial Driving License Jobs

You take pleasure in being out on the wide road. I'm impressed with your driving record. And you're aware that safety is paramount. You may be intent/interested in pursuing a career as just a commercial driver's license (CDL) truck driver. Following Truck Driver Institute, most long-haul truckers travel an average of 500 miles each day and clock an annual mileage of 100,000 - 110,000 miles. Drivers in regional and urban areas travel around 48,000 miles each year. That's a long stretch of highway. To discover which form of CDL driver job is best for you before you enroll in the CDL exam, you must first establish what kind of CDL driver job is best for you.

When you get your commercial driver's license (CDL) via the instruction given by Truck Driving School, you will enjoy several benefits. It can open the door to many interesting prospects that may also prove to be lucrative. You can find a wonderful job almost anyplace if you have a CDL, whether you choose to remain close to home or are prepared to travel. Following are six different sorts of driving jobs that you may earn with a CDL

4.1 Driver of a long-distance cargo truck

The need for truckers who are prepared to carry freight over great distances, whether across the nation or within a particular area, is constantly growing. If you want to have a large effect on the business community in the United States, being a delivery truck driver is an excellent way to do it. When you consider how shipments and commodities are carried throughout the nation from suppliers to consumers, delivery truck drivers are likely connected in some way or another. Whenever someone buys something from Walmart or Amazon or even from a little neighborhood store, they typically depend on truck drivers to get their items to the destination. Pay for these CDL positions is projected to be $30,000 to $35,000 per year. Your geographic area, as well as your past job experience, will decide your salary.

4.2 Bus Driver

You may utilize your CDL to pursue a career as a commercial bus driver. According to the BLS, working on school buses, local transit, or cross-state even cross-country bus routes, one may make a solid income while providing a professional service that is always in great demand.

4.3 Transportation of Heavy Equipment

Not every truck driver transports retail cargo. Many people get their CDLs to move heavy equipment and huge loads on flatbed trucks & trailers. This is a highly specialized sector where safety and training are essential, but it may be rewarding for those prepared to put in the necessary effort.

4.4 Dispatcher

In a nutshell, a dispatcher is indeed a person who communicates with such a truck driver via radio transmissions. You are not needed to drive a vehicle to obtain a CDL. If you've been steering/driving trucks for many years & want to try somewhat else, or if you're just not interested in CDL driver employment, you still have a wide range of options available with your commercial drivers' license. Dispatcher roles enable you to make use of your CDL without needing to take on the responsibilities of a normal truck driver.

In many cases, the dispatcher is responsible for keeping track of trucks and equipment while traveling throughout the country and liaison between truck drivers & carriers. Assisting the driver with any problems that may emerge throughout their travel is also part of their responsibilities. Based on your location and past work experience, the expected compensation range for this CDL position is between $40,000 & $45,000 per year.

Many individuals get their CDLs to work in the sector in positions other than trucking. Being a dispatcher may be a rewarding and fulfilling profession. Rather than driving a huge rig, it plays an important communication function inside a trucking firm. It requires special abilities that can only be learned at a desk while listening to the radio.

In many cases, the dispatcher is responsible for keeping track of trucks and equipment while traveling throughout the country and liaison between truck drivers & carriers. Assisting the driver with any problems that may emerge throughout their travel is also part of their responsibilities. Based on your location and past work experience, the expected compensation range for this CDL position is between $40,000 & $45,000 per year. Become a short-haul driver if you wish to have a shorter operating window, including 12 hours or fewer. Driving over the country's borders is an alternative to driving outside of the country's borders. Short-distance drivers earn a median of $48K a year. Even though this is below long-distance truckers, the benefit of being nearer is substantial.

4.5 Truck driving Instructor

Another non-driving career that is worthwhile to consider is that of a vehicle(truck) driving school instructor. You may put your CDL training and knowledge to work by assisting other aspiring truck drivers in obtaining their commercial driver's licenses and learning via additional advanced and specialized driver training programs and courses.

4.6 Bus Driver

The work of a bus driver is straightforward; they need to convey passengers from one area to another in a secure manner. If you have a CDL (commercial driver's license), you may also operate school buses, workplace buses, mall buses, and even hospital buses. You might also work for a company that provides charter buses or scenic tours. In the United States, the average yearly wage for a bus driver is $30,950.

4.7 Operator/Owner

If you are the owner of a truck or wish to lease from such a carrier, you have the autonomy to pick the sorts of trips you want to do and go at your speed and on your schedule. Consider this to be freelance trucking—looking for assignments that are lucrative or that fit into your daily schedule, your demands, your health requirements, or whatever else you can think of. You are not required to participate in lengthy runs if you do not like to. You get to select which jobs you want to perform and which ones you don't want to do, centered on the size of the car you possess. If you work hard, you might expect to earn up to $150k each year if you are devoted. Of course, you'll have to pay for things like gas, vehicle repairs and maintenance, tire changes, food, and beverages while on the road, and other unanticipated expenditures along the way as well. Even after deducting your yearly expenses, working as a freelance truck driver will still be financially beneficial.

4.8 Terminal Manager

As just the terminal manager, you oversee the smooth functioning of trucking centers, which are locations where freight is loaded & unloaded from trucks. As a terminal manager, you will be accountable/responsible for overseeing the loading and unloading of cargo to minimize damage. Damaged products result in a decrease in turnover and increased customer complaints.

4.9 Driver of a local truck

Looking into more local trucking jobs may be a better option when long-distance driving is not your cup of tea. Depending on your needs, this will be for a delivery truck or other transportation service.

Chapter 5
Overseas CDL

Commercial Driver Licensing laws under federal regulation have been changing, and towns and cities that wish to continue training CDL drivers will have to register with the National Highway Traffic Safety Administration as just a training organization and be subject to the provisions set forth 49 CFR 380. According to the Road Transport Safety Administration, this will become effective in February 2022 and can significantly alter the paradigm by which cities and municipalities develop their demographic of CDL operators for both school buses and public works vehicles, among other things.

More information can be found on the Entry-Level Driver's Education Provider Registry, which can be found here. The registry will assist applicants for commercial driver's licenses in connecting with self-certified training institutions to deliver the entry-level driving instruction required by the state. CDL drivers are subject to alcohol and drug testing standards under 49 CFR 382, which became effective in January 2020 due to a previously passed regulation. For additional information, please see the FMCSA Alcohol and Drug Clearinghouse.

5.1 CDL In the United States

Inside the U. S., the Professional Motor Auto Safety Act. The Act specified basic conditions that must be completed before a state provides a CDL. IN SOME JURISDICTIONS, a CDL could be necessary to operate a motor home or farm vehicle. However, such cars are federally exempted from having to earn a CDL. The following categories of CDL licenses are:

Class A - Allows a cardholder to run combinations of vehicles in trade. It covers vehicles with a Total Combination Addition To considering (GCWR) of renewable energy lbs. (11,794 kg) or even more if the Gross's Weight Capacity (GVWR) of the truck is moreover 10,000 pounds (4,536 kg). Vehicle types that fall within Class A are truck trailers and trailers buses (Passenger certification required) (Passenger endorsement required).

Class B - Enables the cardholder to use heavy passenger vehicles in trade. It comprises cars with a Gross's Weight Ratio (GVWR) of 26,001 kilograms (11,794 kg) or greater. If towing a car, the Gross vehicle weight of the pulled unit must be 10,000 lbs. (4,536 kilograms) or less. Vehicle types under Class B include boxes, delivery, garbage, cement lorries, and busses (Passenger endorsement required) (Passenger endorsement required).

Class C - Allows this same cardholder to function single automobiles of 26,000 lbs. (12,000 kg) a year when the controller plans to travel 16 or more travelers, such as the driver, or is hauling material that's been designated as dangerous under 49 U's code 5103 and therefore is needed to somehow be placarded under subchapter F of 49 C.f.r. Part 172 or is hauling any quantity of a substance mentioned as a then choose agent or toxic substances in 42 CFR Part 73.

State governments decide the age limit for a CDL. In all jurisdictions, including Columbia, the age limit for a License is 18 decades old, apart from Hawaii, where it would be 21 years old. According to the Transportation Security Administration, commercial vehicle drivers must be 21 years old or older to operate a vehicle in interstate commerce.

Although 49 states let 18 to 17-years obtain a CDL, they are only permitted to operate a commercial vehicle inside the state where the CDL was obtained, i.e., in intrastate commerce. Drivers who transport hazardous items and require placards must be 21 years old or older to be eligible to do so. Additional age requirements differ from state to state. After being signed into law on November 15, 2021, the Capital Spending and Jobs Act includes an amendment establishing a three-year apprenticeship program that would allow 18- to 20-year-old kids with a CDL to operate throughout interstate commerce after completing supervised learning with an older and more experienced driver before being allowed to drive in multiple states. When driving commercial automobiles (CMVs), which are mostly trucks (or Longer Combined Vehicles (LCV)), required additional skills and knowledge that were in addition to those needed to drive cars or another light vehicle before 1992; this was known as "commercial truck driving."

Large vehicle and bus drivers were required to obtain a CDL before establishing the CDL in 1992, and licensing criteria varied from the state - to - the state. Because of this absence of training, many preventable road deaths and accidents have occurred. When the Act was passed in 1992, all drivers who operated a business motor vehicle were required to have a business driver's license (CDL). The National Highway Traffic safety administration (FHWA) has created guidelines for evaluating drivers who wish to obtain a driver's license. States in the United States are only permitted to issue CDLs after a practical test has been administered by the Government or an approved testing center. A CDL is required if the vehicle fulfills one specified commercial motor (CMV). A state also may require a CDL for a driver to operate some other types of motor vehicles. For instance, a driver licensed in New Jersey who drives a bus, limo, or van that can be used for hire or intended to carry 8 to 15 people must have a driver's license (CDL). To legally pick up passengers in a bus and other vehicles mentioned in Article carried out with the following of the Government's Motor and Traffic Law, a driver's license in Manhattan must be held by a driver's license. If driving is their principal source of income, drivers licensed in California must hold a driver's license (CDL), regardless of whether they operate a business vehicle. In California, a commercial vehicle is defined as transports persons or goods for hire regularly. Additionally, in California, having a driver's license lowers the threshold for receiving a Driving Underneath the Effect citation from 0.08 percent to 0.04 percent blood alcohol level. Prospective licensees should check their state's CDL requirements by consulting its CDL Manual.

5.2 CDL In the United Kingdom

Depending on the bearer's type of Professional Driving Test, it is possible to drive busses and minibusses in the United Kingdom with a PCV License (PCV stands for Passengers Carrying Vehicle).

Category C+E - vehicles are weighing more than 3,500 kilograms (7,700 lb.) with a trailer weighing more than 750 kilograms (1,650 lb.), also recognized as Large Goods Vehicles, with a normal maximum gross weight of 44,000 kilograms (97,000 lb.): driver must be at least 21 years old, 17 if in the Armed Forces, and now 18 if the driver meets certain CPC requirements.

Drivers in Category D1- are permitted to operate vehicles with between eight and sixteen passenger seats and a trailer with a limit permissible mass of 750 kilograms (1,650 lb.) or less.

Category D1+E- the holder may drive a vehicle that has between nine and 16 passenger seats while towing a trailer that weighs more than 750 kilograms (1,650 lb.) maximum authorization mass, given that the highest authorized mass of something like the trailer doesn't exceed the fully laden volume of the vehicle of been driven and that the merged maximum authorized material of the vehicle and recreational vehicle does not surpass 12,000 kilograms (22,400 lb.) (26,000 lb.). As an example, a vehicle including a fully laden mass of 2,650 kilograms (5,840 pounds) and a maximum allowable mass (MAM) of 4,005 kilograms (8,830 pounds), in combination with a trailer with a maximum allowable mass of 2,200 kilograms (4,900 pounds), will result in a merged MAM of 6,205 kilograms (13,680 pounds) - and the fully laden mass of the car being driven (2,650 kilograms (5,840 pounds)) is greater

The combined MAM of a vehicle with just an unladen volume of 2,650 kilograms (5,840 lb.) as well as a MAM of the 4,005 kilograms (8,830 lb.), plus a trailer with a MAM of 2,700 kilograms (6,000 lb.), will be 6,705 kilograms (14,782 lb.) - or because the Mother of the wagon (2,700 kilograms (6,000 lb.)) surpasses the unladen mass of the vehicle becoming driven. Drivers of vehicles with more than seven-passenger seats are permitted to tow trailers weighing up to 750 kilograms (1,650 lb.) maximum allowable mass following Category D.

Category D+E - permits the licensee to operate a vehicle with seven-passenger seats while towing a trailer weighing more than 750 kilograms (1,650 lb.) of maximum permissible mass.

5.3 CDL In Australia

The driver license system in Australia is largely the same throughout the country, while significant differences exist between states and territories (for example, what classes of license are available). C Car: A 'Category C' license is valid for cars with a gross vehicle (GVM) of up to 4.5 tons (4.4 long tons; 5.0 short tons). The GVM is the recommended maximum weight when a vehicle is fully loaded. Those with a Class C license can operate automobiles, public utility vehicles, vans, commercial vehicles, motor trikes, tractors, and agricultural implements, including such graders. You can also operate vehicles that can accommodate up to 12 passengers, including the driver.

R Rider- Motorcyclists must have a 'Category R' license.

LR Light Rigid- A stiff vehicle with a gross vehicle mass (GVM) of more than 4.5 tons (4.4 long tons; 5.0 short tons) but not more than 8 tons is classified as a 'Class LR' vehicle. Any towed trailer shall not weigh upwards of 9 tons gross vehicle weight (GVW) (8.9 long tons: 9.9 short tons). 'C' class vehicles are also included in this category, as are vehicles with a gross vehicle weight rating of up to 8 tons (7.9 long tons; 8.8 short tons) that carry other than 12 persons, including the driver, and automobiles in class 'C. Any towed trailer shall not weigh over 9 tons gross vehicle weight (GVW) (8.9 long tons: 9.9 short tons).

HR Heavy Rigid- A rigid motor vehicle with three or more axles and a gross vehicle mass (GVM) greater than eight tons is classified as a 'Class HR' vehicle. Any towed trailer shall not weigh over 9 tons gross vehicle weight (GVW) (8.9 long tons: 9.9 short tons). This class comprises articulated busses and vehicles in the 'MR' classification. Large combination vehicles, such as a prime mover pulling a semi-trailer or a rigid vehicle pulling a trailer, are covered by this license, with a gross vehicle weight rating (GVM) of more than 9 tons. This class comprises automobiles classified as 'HR.' A vehicle licensed under this category includes multi-combination vehicles such as road trains or B-Double vehicles. It also includes automobiles of the 'HC' classification.

The Public Transport Authority and Aust roads establish medical requirements for commercial vehicle drivers, detailed in 'Assessing Fitness to Drive,' available. It is strongly suggested that applicants for large vehicle license categories MR (Medium Rigid), HR (Large Rigid), HC (Heavy Combination), or MC (Multi Combination) confirm that they meet all medical requirements before beginning any training or examinations for a heavy vehicle license. For a vehicle transporting paying customers (such as a bus or tourist coach), the driver must have an appropriate driver's license and a 'Public Passenger Car Driver Authority,' provided by the Department of Transport.

5.4: CDL In New Zealand

The New Zealand Transport Agency (NZTA) oversees driver licensing. There are six different motor vehicle licenses and nine diverse types of license endorsements. Vehicles with a GLW (gross loaded weight) and GCW (gross combination weight) of less than 6,000 kg are classified as Class 1, whereas motorbikes are classified as Class 6. Heavy vehicles are governed by classes 2–5.

A Class 2 permit permits the holder may drive in the following situations: The term "rigid vehicle" refers to any vehicle (along with any tractor) with a gross vehicle weight (GVW) greater than 6,000 kilograms (13,000 lb.) but a little less than 18,001 kilograms (39,685 lb.). Any combination vehicle has a gross combined weight (GCW) of less than 12,000 kilograms (26,000 lb.). In addition, any combination vehicle that is composed of a rigid car with a gross vehicle weight (GVW) of 18,000 kilograms (40,000 lb.) or less hauling a light trailer (GVW of 3,500 kilograms (7,700 lb.) or less is prohibited. Any inflexible vehicle with a gross vehicle weight (GVW) of more than 18,000 kilograms (40,000 lb.) and no and over two axles is considered heavy. Any vehicle that falls under the purview of Class 1.

Class 3 permits the holder to drive in the following situations: Any combination car with a GCW of greater than 12,000 kilograms (26,000 lbs.) but less than 25,001 kilograms is considered a combination vehicle (55,118 lb.). Any vehicle that falls under the purview defined earlier, and 2. Class 4 permits the bearer to drive in the following situations: Any rigid equipment (including any tractor) having a gross vehicle weight rating (GVWR) of more than 18,000 kg (40,000 lb.). Any combination vehicle is comprised of a rigid truck with a gross vehicle weight (GVW) of further than 18,000 kilograms (40,000 lb.) hauling a light trailer (with a GVW of less than 3,500 kilograms (7,700 lb.). Automobiles fall under classes 1 & 2 but not under class 3. Class 5 permits the holder's license to drive in the following situations. Any combination vehicle has A gross combined weight (GCW) greater than 25,000 kilograms (55,000 lb.). Vehicles fall under classes 1, 2, 3, and 4.

5.5: CDL In Hong Kong

The New Zealand Transport Agency (NZTA) oversees driver licensing. There are six different motor vehicle licenses [19] and nine diverse types of license endorsements. Vehicles with a GLW (gross loaded weight) and GCW (gross combination weight) of less than 6,000 kg are classified as Class 1, whereas motorbikes are classified as Class 6.

Heavy vehicles are governed by classes 2–5. The Class 2 license permits the holder can drive in the following situations: The term "rigid vehicle" refers to any vehicle (such as any tractor) with a gross vehicle weight (GVW) greater than 6,000 kilograms (13,000 lb.) but much less than 18,001 kilograms (39,685 lb.). Any combination vehicle has a gross combined weight (GCW) of less than 12,000 kilograms (26,000 lb.). In addition, any combination vehicle that is composed of a rigid car with a gross vehicle weight (GVW) of 18,000 kilograms (40,000 lb.) or less hauling a light trailer (GVW of 3,500 kilograms (7,700 lb.) or less is prohibited. Any rigid truck with a gross vehicle weight (GVW) of 18,000 kilograms (40,000 lb.) and no or more two axles is considered a heavy vehicle. Any vehicle that falls under the purview of Class 1. Class 3 permits the bearer to drive in the following situations: Any combination vehicle with a GCW of greater than 12,000 kilograms (26,000 lb.) but less than 25,001 kilograms is considered a combination vehicle (55,118 lb.). Any vehicle that falls under the purview of classes 1 through 2. Class 4 permits the bearer to drive in the following situations. Any rigid vehicle (along with any tractor) having a gross vehicle weight rating (GVWR) of more than 18,000 kg (40,000 lb.)

Any combination vehicle is comprised of a rigid truck with a gross vehicle weight (GVW) of more exceeding 18,000 kilograms (40,000 lb.) hauling a light trailer (with a GVW of less than 3,500 kilograms (7,700 lb.). Automobiles fall under classes 1 & 2 but not under class 3. Class 5 permits the holder's license to drive in the following situations. Any combination vehicle had a gross combined weight (GCW) greater than 25,000 kilograms (55,000 lb.). Vehicles fall under classes 1, 2, 3, and 4.

5.6: Is Overseas Trucking and CDL The Right Career Path for You?

Although many truck drivers choose to work for local corporations, foreign drivers prefer to pursue careers in other nations. To assist you in preparing for your first driving truck job, here is a glance at several indicators that international trucking is the correct choice for you.

5.7: You Are Attentive in Learning About Other Cultures

The desire to learn about various cultures and languages is one of the most telling signals that you are suited for an international truck driving profession.

When you work in another country, you will become completely absorbed in the country's customs, regulations, and way of life. Trucking employment in foreign countries, such as retail truck jobs in Europe or delivery trucking jobs within the Middle East, provides an opportunity to learn about and experience various other cultures.

5.8: You Are Not Intimidated by The Prospect of Higher Criteria

To be deemed for a truck taking the position in another nation, you may need to demonstrate your willingness to take additional tests and pass licensing exams.

Depending on your nation of choice, it may be essential to secure a work permit for the period you'll be working in the country of your choice. If you are not bothered by the additional requirements, international employment as a truck driver could be a terrific next step in your career.

5.9: You Are Fluent in Another Language

Working as a commercial trucker in another nation will give you an excellent opportunity to improve your foreign language proficiency. Even if you grew up knowing two languages or have only recently begun studying another, you will have lots of opportunities to put your newfound knowledge to use as soon as you begin working in your chosen nation.

Following are the countries in which getting a CDL is easy.

Australia

The trucking industry in Australia is thriving at an unprecedented rate. Contrary to widespread belief, an

Australian driver's average wage can be as high as $1 million (USD), which rises if items are transported from one state to the other. If you drive a long-haul truck over state lines, your annual compensation could reach $100,000 (USD).

Norway

In addition to providing excellent job opportunities for truck drivers, Norway's strong economic structure provides excellent job prospects for people working in various other fields. Drivers of trucks work five weeks a week for no and over 7 - 8 hours per day, and the average yearly wage for a trucker is $58,000. (USD). When it comes to earning potential, truckers can earn $90,000 (USD) each year if they are ready to work additional hours.

The United States of America

Because the American economy is heavily reliant on delivering products and services, the demand for truck drivers is always increasing. Truckers are in high demand in the United States, which has a thriving trucking industry that is predicted to develop dramatically in the future years. Truck drivers in the U.s earn an average wage of approximately $53,000 per year. The nicest aspect of becoming a commercial truck driver is that you may start as early as you want and that you wouldn't need a bachelor's degree to get started in the industry.

The country of Canada

According to Forbes, Canada, one of the world's most open and varied countries, is a hotspot for business start-ups and the trucking industry.

Truck drivers are well compensated for their efforts when it comes to shipping. The average yearly wage was $56,000 (USD), while if you choose to work as a local grab and deliver trucker, you can expect to earn approximately $1 million (USD) in a single year of employment. Your pay in Canada is also determined by the amount of trucking experience you have. If you decide to become a lengthy truck driver, your annual income might surpass $100,000. (USD).

Switzerland

Although Switzerland ranks among the loveliest countries on the planet, it must have continued several of the top nations globally for truck drivers. As a foreigner working within Switzerland, you can expect to make an annual salary of $64,000 on average (USD). However, based on your expertise, work hours, and type of vehicle, you can make up to $90,000 (USD), though the distance traveled is a significant factor in deciding your earnings.

The country of Sweden

The average yearly wage of a truck driver in Sweden can reach $33,000 (USD), and the country is home to two of the world's largest truck manufacturing enterprises. Because the trucking industry is so large, truckers are unquestionably an asset to the country.

Netherlands

A prosperous country with a large economy, the Netherlands ranks 17th in its largest economies, making it one of the world's wealthiest countries. But if you're a trucker, you will have a plethora of employment choices in this nation, and you can expect an annual pay that is somewhat higher than $40,000 on average (USD).

Chapter 6

Requirements for CDL

The federal government imposes the fundamental standards for the various kinds of commercial driver's licenses, but states are free to impose extra restrictions that they see appropriate.

According to federal law, if you want to drive commercially over state lines, you must be 21 years old or older. Many states, however, will only give a CDL for intrastate driving to persons who are 18 years old or older; see your state's requirements for more information.

The following documents will be required when you can apply for the commercial driver's license and have completed the CDL application form for your state: your security number, proof of identification, and evidence of residence in the state where you want to work.

In most states, your social security voucher, a Medicare Identity card, an existing I.D. card from any division of the US Armed Forces (athletically inclined, retired, reserve, or completely reliant), or a military detachment document, also known as a DD-214, are all acceptable forms of identification to prove your social security number. Check with your state to see whether they accept any other kinds of identification as verification of your social security number. The list of papers that may be used to prove your identification varies even more from State to State. For example, a valid U.S. birth cert or certified copy of a valid U.S. birth certificate, a valid U.S. passport, a valid USCIS American Indian Card, a valid military I.D. card, a certificate either of Citizenship or Naturalization, a Permanent Resident Card, or a Temporary Resident ID Card are all acceptable forms of identification. Probably, your state recognizes a variety of additional papers as identification, so it's advisable to consult your State's CDL handbook or DMV webpage for the most up-to-date information.

Your obligation also delivers evidence that you are medically capable of driving professionally. It is in addition to supplying documentation of your forename, birth date, county of residence, age, your social security card. A vision test, which you will do in connection with the implementation of your CDL examinations, will be the most straightforward part of this procedure; nevertheless, the more involved aspect will need you to provide appropriate medical records. The Exam Conditions Report Form and the Medical Examiner's Certificate Form will be required to be submitted to your state business driver's license agency beginning in 2022, regardless of whether you are driving intrastate or interstate. Suppose you want to drive over state lines. In that case, you must have your medical documents filled out by a medical examiner who is certified by the National Registry for Certified Medical Examiners. If these documents are necessary for your work duties, your employer is responsible for covering their cost.

After submitting all required papers, you must pass the required examinations. All commercial driver's licenses candidates must pass a sight examination and a learning examination. You will be issued a commercial learner's permit if you have passed these tests (CLP). According to the Federal regulations, you must have a CLP for at least 14 days since you may sit for your road skills exam. (Some jurisdictions may mandate a longer term of keeping.) A CLP may be valid once per year nonrenewable, or it may be valid for much less than a year and renewable, depending on the state that issued it. It is important to note that your possible company may include extra criteria on the application form to attract CDL drivers with the highest levels of credentials.

If you wish to work as a truck driver, you must understand the CDL criteria for obtaining a CDL (commercial driver's license) before applying. In addition, the same requirements apply to the CLP, or commercial learner's permit, which you'll need to practice before you can get a commercial driver's license. The federal CDL standards (described below) apply to all 50 states in the United States. Then it would help if you investigated the CDL criteria in your state. Each jurisdiction has its minimal qualifications for obtaining a commercial driver's license, and these standards vary from one state to the next. There are a variety of prerequisites for earning a commercial driver's license, all of which could differ from State to State:

- An existing driver's license is required. Drivers who want to earn a CDL license must first have a valid non-commercial driver's license.
- There is an age requirement. Drivers' requirement is at minimum 18 years old to get a commercial driver's license (CDL) and at minimum 21 years old to carriage hazardous items over state boundaries.
- Driver's license history. Before obtaining their commercial driver's licenses, drivers should have one to 2 years of driving experience. It is prohibited for their driving records to include suspensions due to things like earning driving points, traffic offenses, DUIs/DWIs, refusing to show up in court, or refusing to pay child support. Drivers who have their licenses suspended must stay from traveling for a certain time, take a safety course, and pay reinstatement costs.
- There is no criminal record. Drivers must be able can pass a background check before being hired.

- Proof of citizenship is required. To drive, drivers must be able to provide proof of citizenship, such as a national insurance number or birth certificate, always.
- Comprehension of the English language. Drivers must be capable of reading and speaking English well to operate their vehicles.
- Physical and medical norms should be met. To drive, drivers must possess a valid Medical Examiner's Certificate, which certifies that they have acceptable visual and health conditions.

6.1 Training Requirements

The FMCSA has made several adjustments to its regulations' "compliance requirements" section. The FMCSA was established to make U.S. roadways safer, primarily through reducing commercial truck-related accidents, as its name indicates. Since the passage of the Commercial Vehicle Safety Acts of 1986, drivers have been prohibited from holding a commercial driver's license in more than a State. It stopped the practice of drivers obtaining several driver's licenses to conceal any criminal convictions they may have in a previous state.

Hazardous Materials Approval Requirements Have Been Revised

States were obligated to begin applying the texting limit regulation in late 2013.

Later, beginning in 2014, professional drivers were required to "choose and self-certify" their medical information. They were only permitted to utilize "approved" medical examiners listed on the Leading Medical Registry.

How Long Would It Take you Train for a Commercial Driver's License (CDL)?

CDL license training may be completed in as little as one year at a vocational school, often less time-consuming than a four-year college. The Delta Technical School CDL Training Course may be completed in only 168 hours over 20 days, with evening and day sessions available. The coursework is divided into the following sections:

- Week 1: The first week is expended in the classroom, familiarizing students with Mississippi CDL knowledge, driving security, air brakes, pairing vehicles, logbooks, route planning, and policy and employee relations. Week 2: The second week is expended in the classroom, familiarizing students with Mississippi CDL knowledge, driving security, air brakes, pairing vehicles, logs, route planning, and general populace and employee relations.

- Weeks 2-4: The next weeks of the program will be spent on the range, on the road, and in remedial training, in which participants will be analyzing and interpreting system control data. In addition, they will learn about pre-trip regular inspections, post-trip vehicle situation reports, switch execution, backing, parking, and docking processes, coupling and disentangling trailers, trying to manage and making adjustments vehicle speed, trying to manage and adjust car space relations, identify possible driving hazards, going to perform emergency maneuvers, identifying and making adjustments to extreme driving situations, planning trips, recording/maintaining hours, and planning trips and maintaining hours.

Students interested in gaining more in-depth driving a truck experience may participate in the Delta Tech Professionals Truck Driving Program*, which needs about 600 clock hours over 20 weeks.

People spent 300 hours of classroom teaching, 24 hours on the range for observation, 24 hours on the road, and 252 hours in remedial instruction throughout the program. This program is offered at Delta Tech in both day and evening sessions. The following are the sections of the Expert Truck Driving coursework:

- Weeks 1-4: During the first month, students receive the necessary understanding of CDL permit test prep, CDL approval preparation (pairs and tankers), vehicle maintenance for everyday operations and safe practices, and contaminants (hazmat) training. Weeks 5-8: During the second month, students receive the necessary knowledge on CDL license test preparation, CDL acknowledgment preparation (doubles/triples and tankers), and contaminants (hazmat) training.
- Weeks 5-12: The second month of the curriculum includes vehicle inspection for everyday operation and safety procedures. Weeks 5-12: Students will learn how to interpret and recognize instrument control systems in this lesson. The fundamentals of truck control, coupling and disentangling, range maneuvers, road training, days of service/logging, route planning/map interpretation, communication, receiving, and health are all covered in the lessons. In addition, the training provides information on defensive driving, danger awareness, and driving in adverse weather situations.

- Weeks 13-20: During the final two weeks of the program, students learn regarding vehicle inspection, forklift mentoring, load securement/cargo ability to handle, preventative maintenance, Federal Motor Carrier Safety Administration (FMCSA) rules, and regulations, weigh channels, transportation protection, ELDT (entry-level driving lessons), company speaking, resume building, road life, and professionalism/soft skills. Students get instruction in preparation for the state range and driving exam during this period.

Delta Tech's truck driver training programs prepare students to take and pass the CDL Class A licensure examination. CDL Class A licenses enable drivers to operate any mix of vehicles with a combined weight of 26,001 pounds or more, excluding Class B and C vehicles, if they have the appropriate endorsements.

6.2 Health and Physical Requirements

According to the sort of driving a trucker does, the physical requirements of his profession are different. However, regardless of the kind, a driver must be physically fit, operate a corporate motor vehicle, and do the many non-driving trucking responsibilities required. It involves dealing with extended stretches of transportation, unpredictable sleep habits, possible family and social issues, and job-related stressors like deadlines. Aside from that, some positions need heavy lifting during the loading and unloading process, bending, and bending, climbing into or out of the vehicle many times per day, putting tire chains on an as-needed basis (depending on where you work), and a variety of other physically demanding duties.

You must have the original or photojournalism copy of this document while operating an advertising motor vehicle, as required by the United States Department of Transportation. While operating an advertising motor vehicle, you must have the original or digital images copy in your possession.

CDL Self-Certification

Commercial drivers will be required to "self-certify" their medical information beginning in 2014. They will only be permitted to employ "approved" forensic experts listed on the Leading Medical Registry. Visit this page to locate a pathologist the Federal Motor Carrier Safety Administration has qualified to do DOT physical examinations.

All commercial drivers are now required to self-certify the kind of vehicle they intend to operate in each of the categories listed below:

- It implies that you must fulfill the Federal Department of Transportation medical card standards to operate across state boundaries on non-exempted Interstate routes.
- Excepted Interstate: You are exempt from meeting the Federal Department of Transportation's medical card criteria if you operate across state boundaries.
- Non-Excepted Intrastate: One must fulfill a Federal Department of Transportation medical card's standards and only operate inside your home state.
- Intrastate exception: You are not required to fulfill the National DOT medical exemption criteria if you are operating inside your home state.

Physical Requirements for Commercial Drivers at a Fundamental Level

The Medical Examination for Commercial Drivers Fitness Assessment is a Federal Motor Carrier Safety Administration (FMCSA) document that medical examiners utilize. This form and the whole list that can be found lower down on that page will offer you an attired sense of the medical credentials required for drivers. You will now be needed to get a "Medical Examiner's Certificate" to demonstrate that you are medically competent in driving a professional motor vehicle under certain conditions. A few of the prerequisites include the following:

- The acuity of at least 20/40 (Snellen) in each eye, with or without correction, is considered acceptable. Each eye must have at minimum of 70 degrees of peripheral vision in the horizontal meridian. Proper vision correction is possible using spectacles or contact lenses. The use of vision correction should be recorded on the Medical Examiner's Certificate, although it is not required.
- You are unable to be diabetic and need insulin injections with a needle. Please keep in mind that certain motorists may be exempt from this requirement.

- Hearing: The standard is as follows: a) Must first detect a forced whispered voice at a distance more than 5 feet, with or without a hearing aid, or b) must have an annual hearing loss in the better ear of fewer than 40 decibels.
- Blood Pressure: He does not have a current medical assessment of hypertension that would impair his ability to drive a commercial motorized vehicle appropriately.
- Elevated Blood Glucose Levels: A blood sugar level of 200 or more is deemed "dangerous." However, even though many other websites have stated that having a blood sugar level of 200 or above is a disqualification, there seems to be no evidence to back this claim. Other medical disorders, such as sleep aponia, could also be a disqualifying factor.

Emergency Procedures for COVID-19

Because of the COVID-19 pandemic (new coronavirus) pandemic, its National Highway Traffic Safety Administration (FMCSA) recently announced a set of Emergency Declarations to help the nation's commerce respond more effectively to the emergency posed by this pandemic. These declarations have resulted in exemptions from some of the standard standards for commercial transportation, such as the ones listed below:

- States are permitted to extend the validity of CLPs for some time of more than one year.
- When holding a CLP, the bearer is not obliged to wait a minimum of 14 days until completing the CDL driving skills exam.

- A CLP or CDL shall remain valid even if the holder's medical certificate or health variance has expired at the time of issuance of the license.

As the COVID-19 situation has lasted, FMCSA has extended or changed these and other crisis regulations.

6.3 Written and Knowledge-Based Examinations

To get a commercial driver's license, you must pass knowledge and skills examinations. The CDL guidebook will assist you in passing the state examinations. This guidebook is not intended to serve as a replacement for a truck driver's education class or program.

Professional education is the most dependable approach to master the numerous skills necessary for safely operating a big commercial vehicle and achieving the status of a good driver in the trucking business. Formal training may be obtained via a variety of sources.

Testing on the Job and the Road

For the road and abilities test, you must utilize the same commercial vehicle category that you want to use to get a license for the commercial vehicle.

The three-part driving exam consists of the following components:

Pre-trip car inspection – You must know that your vehicle is okay to drive before going out on your journey. It is covered in detail in CDL Manual parts 11, 12, and 13 on how you must describe what you are checking and why you are inspecting it.

Control of a vehicle at its most fundamental level - You will be evaluated on your ability to maintain control of your car. It comprises the vehicle's movement ahead, backward, and inside a set region, among other things.

You will be required to show your ability to safely operate a commercial car on the road in various traffic circumstances during your on-road driving examination. Left and right movements, stops, sweeping bends, railroad crossings, etc.)

Waiver of Military Obligations

Did you at least drive a CMV (or even a commercial motor vehicle) while serving in the armed forces? You may be eligible to avoid taking the skills test section of the professional driver's license skills exam if you meet certain requirements. Military drivers must submit their applications within one year after being released from active service.

This form can be used by serving people who are presently licensed and are or were engaged within the past 90 days in service employment requiring a military moving vehicle equal to a Commercial Heavy Truck (CMV) (CMV). This waiver permits a qualifying military member to apply for a commercial driver's license (CDL) without undergoing skills testing. It is impossible to waive the CDL knowledge (written) test(s). School Bus (S) and Passenger (P) certifications obtained via this Waiver Program may not be transferred to another individual or entity.

Chapter 7

Endorsements

Contingent to your state's obligations, you may be required to obtain extra endorsements in addition to a commercial driver's license. Consider the following scenario: if you intend to work in a job where you will be responsible for transporting hazardous chemicals, you may be required to pass exams again for H endorsements.

In the alternative, if you intend to work as a bus driver, you may require the S certification, which involves completing an examination and a road test. Several other endorsements are tasks, like the X or endorsements for tank trucks and hazardous operations, which are examples of this. The Endorsement will almost certainly necessitate completing a skills test and a road test for each instance. There are multiple kinds of CDL licenses and endorsements available. It can be difficult to decide which one is top for you without determining your needs and potential employment requirements. To avoid legal peril for driving a vehicle without a proper license, conduct thorough research before getting behind the wheel. Although, if you find by hand in this situation, you can always seek the advice of an attorney.

CDL Classes A Endorsement deals are classified into six categories.

7.1 (H) Hazardous Substances and Materials (HAZMAT)

A HAZMAT certification enables you to transport hazardous items across the road safely and efficiently. This employment is frequently more lucrative, and there is typically a greater pool of accessible positions. Once you have obtained your CDL A, you can apply for a HAZMAT endorsement after passing the necessary TSA background checks, passing a written test, and passing a medical exam conducted by a DOT doctor. In many circumstances, having your HAZMAT license is a condition for obtaining the X endorsement, which will be discussed in greater detail later. To operate a vehicle carrying placarded hazardous items, you must have an H endorsement on your license (hazmat's). To be qualified to apply, you must be a citizen of the United States, a legal resident, or possess a valid Work Authorization Document. You must first pass a comprehensive knowledge exam to be eligible for this Endorsement.

7.2 (N) Tank Transport Vehicle

The tank endorsement authorizes a driver to transport a tank, sometimes known as a "tanker," containing liquid or gaseous elements. These occupations are typically higher-paying and are usually local or regional, allowing you to spend more time at home than you would with certain other jobs. However, this Endorsement necessitates the completion of an extra written test. If the tanker is not filled, a tank truck driver must be able to react to the fact that his cargo is continually moving around. The ability to deal with the "surge" created by the displacement of the water in the tank when driving takes some time and effort to master. An N endorsement is required to drive a tank vehicle, defined as a vehicle that transports liquids in a tank. You must first pass a written learning exam to be eligible for this Endorsement.

7.3 (P) Transportation of Passengers

The approval process for passenger transportation is rather basic. It allows a licensed driver to operate a vehicle that transports over 16 passengers, such as a city transit bus. You must pass an additional written and skills test to acquire this Endorsement. Individuals who wish to drive on a scheduled schedule and return home each night or who want to experience the country while driving for travel businesses will find these occupations ideal. One thing is certain: you will be in constant contact with passengers throughout the day, so this is not a career for somebody who prefers to be alone. This Endorsement is typically required to earn the S endorsement, which is required to drive kids in a school bus. Typically, both S & P certifications go hand in hand. A P certification is required to run a vehicle with seating for 16 or more people involving the driver. You must have an acceptable driver's license until today (for instance, no DWI, reckless drive, high speed, or other serious offenses). To obtain this Endorsement, you must first pass an oral knowledge test, followed by a road skills examination.

7.4 (S) Bus Transportation Services

School bus endorsement is required for anyone who wishes to transport children in school buses. This, as though the P endorsement previously stated, necessitates the completion of an additional written or driving skills test. However, additional requirements for the S endorsement include vetting, criminal history checks, and fitness and strength tests. They are typically required to undergo more regular extra training and testing when school bus regulations change. Furthermore, these motorists should have more tolerance and should be able to accept driving youngsters who are a nuisance. Or double-triple trailers are required to have their approval. The T endorsement permits drivers to tow and over one trailer just on the rear of their truck with the help of the T endorsement. This Endorsement also necessitates the completion of an additional written test. Using the T endorsement, a driver can haul double or three times the freight they could come with a normal trailer while traveling the same length over the road. These trucking jobs are frequently more lucrative because of the additional expertise and driving aptitude that the driver must possess. Although an S certification is required on a school bus, it is necessary to first obtain a P endorsement to be eligible to apply. If you incur driving violations like speeding or crossing the opposite side of the street, you may forfeit your privilege to drive with the S endorsement. To obtain this Endorsement, you must first pass a theoretical knowledge test, followed by a road skills examination. In addition, your state will carry out checks on you before issuing the Endorsement to you.

7.5 (X) Tank and Dangerous Materials Transport

Lastly, the X endorsement enables a driver to transport significant amounts of any form of liquid or gas HAZMAT material within the confines of a tanker vehicle. Having that X endorsement distinguishes these drivers and particular skill sets from the rest. An additional written examination is required for this Endorsement. If drivers intend to work in the oil and gas transportation industry, they will probably need an X endorsement. This Endorsement is a mix of H and N, which allows you to carry hazardous items in a tank. To be considered, you must meet the H and N endorsement standards. You must first pass an oral knowledge exam to be eligible for this Endorsement. Regardless of the sort of license and certifications you pursue, you must guarantee that you are paired with the best-fitting employment for your skills and experience. Drive My Way can assist you whether you are a newly licensed skilled/professional truck driver seeking your first road job or a seasoned veteran who has been driving for a lot of years. We can connect you with the ideal employment for you.

7.6 T-Signal Endorsement

You'll need a T endorsement on your license to pull double or triple trailers. You must first pass an oral knowledge exam to be eligible for this Endorsement.

7.7 CDL Restrictions

There are numerous types of restrictions associated with your CDL. Each limitation prevents the operation of specific commercial motor vehicles (CMVs). These limits apply to all 50 states in the United States; however, there may be extra restrictions depending on where you live.

Driving commercial motor vehicles (CMVs) is challenging, and there are numerous rules that you must be aware of. Most of the limits listed below will be imposed on your CDL since you passed the CDL driving skills in a vehicle that lacked the necessary equipment to pass the test. For example, suppose you pass your driving test in a commercial motor vehicle with an automatic gearbox.

In that case, you will be issued an E limitation that prevents you from driving a commercial motor vehicle with a manual gearbox. Commercial Driver Licenses/Permits may be subject to additional restrictions depending on the type of car and equipment that the driver utilizes for the skills test. It is important to remember that Commercial Learner's Permits are restricted to only showing the Passenger, School Bus, and Tank vehicle endorsements in addition to the restrictions listed below.

7.8 Restriction on E

An E limitation prevents the driver from operating a commercial motor vehicle equipped with a manual gearbox. The driver is only permitted to operate a commercial motor vehicle with an automatic car in other circumstances. The driver is prohibited from operating automobiles with manual gearboxes due to this limitation.

If you complete the basic skills test or road driver's test with a manual gearbox rather than an automatic transmission, you can have this restriction lifted. Avoid taking your driving exams in a vehicle with an automatic gearbox since the chances of your employers, which has automatic gearbox automobiles are extremely low.

7.9 Restriction (F)

An F limitation implies that the driver could only operate commercial motor vehicles (CMVs) with dual outside mirrors. When a driver is physically unable to move their head, is constitutionally blind in one eye, or has impaired hearing, the driver is placed in this category. The twin outside mirrors will be of assistance in that they will show a bigger area from around the vehicle.

7.10 Restriction (G)

A G limitation indicates that the driver is only licensed to run the CMV throughout daylight hours only. On the physician's recommendation, the G limitation is imposed on drivers who have poor eyesight, commonly defined as having eyesight of less than 50/50 in eyes.

7.11 Restriction on K's

When an applicant is under 21, several states impose a K restriction on their application. It denotes that the bearer is only licensed to operate within the state and that they are not permitted to drive outside state lines. When the CDL holder reaches the age of 21, this limitation should be lifted. This is the only Restriction that applies within a state.

This means that the motorist is only permitted to drive inside the state's boundaries in which they received their CDL. With this Restriction, commercial vehicle drivers are not permitted to drive over state lines. If you intend to drive between other states, you must avoid this Restriction as much as possible.

7.12 L Restriction Is a Restriction That Applies to A Person

Both the L restriction and the Z restriction have the same effect in that they both ban the operator from operating commercial motor vehicles (CMV) fitted with massive air brakes.

If you make a mistake when checking the air brake during the road written exam, you will be awarded an L limitation if you cannot correctly identify the entire air brake system or fail your air brakes knowledge test.

Drivers who operate vehicles equipped with a total air brake pedal are prohibited from doing so under these conditions. This occurs when one of the following events occurs:

1. You do not pass the written examination for the air brakes endorsement.

2. Fail the component of the before vehicle test that involves the air brakes.

3. Pass the road driver's test in a company truck that doesn't have a fully functional air brake system.

You may be required to pass an airbag written test, a pre-trip inspection, and the basic skills or driving tests using a vehicle with either a full or partial steering system to be released from this Restriction.

7.13 Restriction on The Use M

An M limitation implies that the driver is only permitted to operate buses or private cars in the Class B and C categories. This Restriction is imposed when a driver earns the traveler bus endorsement while driving a Class B vehicle. This signifies that the driver has a Class A commercial driver's license, but they obtained their passengers or educational bus endorsement while driving a Class B vehicle. This means that the driver will be subject to the "M" limitation, which will limit their ability to operate a passenger car or school bus to just Class B and Class C vehicles.

7.14 N Restriction

Class C helps schools and drivers exclude passenger vehicles from operation subject to an N restriction. This Restriction is imposed when a driver earns the passenger/school buses endorsement while driving a Class C vehicle. The N limitation indicates that the driver has a Class B commercial driver's license but acquired their bus or student endorsement while driving a Class C car. This means that the operator is only permitted to operate a Class C standard car or a school bus in this situation.

7.15 O Restriction

An O limitation prevents a driver from operating a commercial motor vehicle with a fourth connection. Drivers who pass the CDL road knowledge test in a commercial motor vehicle (CMV) without employing a fifth-wheel attachment or pintle hook will be subject to the O limitation.

It signifies that the driver has completed the fundamental skills and highway driving exam but has not driven a semi-trailer or tow truck as part of their qualification. The driver will not be permitted to operate a semi-trailer till they have passed the basic skills & road driving exam in a quasi or truck-trailer vehicle. The motorist was not operating a vehicle equipped with a travel trailer.

7.16 V Restriction

A V restriction is placed on their driving privilege when a driver has a medicinal variance reported to the FMCSA, such as eyesight or poor hearing, seizure, or diabetes. A copy of their Medical Examiner's Certificate must be presented to the DMV to have your commercial driver's license (CDL) amended if you have an existing medical deviation not included on your current driver's license.

This is the most recent CDL restriction to be implemented. When you have completed your DOT physical test, and the doctor determines that your license requires a medical waiver, you should seek legal counsel. A health waiver is frequently required for people with diabetes, people who have hearing problems, people who have seizures, and people who have vision problems, and the waiver are sent directly from the coroner's office to the DMV. Typically, the DMV cannot receive a copy of this; instead, you must have it submitted directly from the examiner to the DMV. If you have a health variance, you will be required to get the V limitation on your commercial driver's license.

7.17 Restriction X

Holders of a Commercial Learner's Permit are the only ones subject to an X limitation. It means that the tank vehicle must be empty, and the tanks must always be purged of all contents.

7.18 Restriction on the Z

A Z restriction prevents the driver from operating commercial motor vehicles (CMVs) without full air brakes. Although most commercial motor vehicles (CMVs) are fitted with air brakes because of their greater braking efficiency, you may still be subject to this limit if you pass a CDL road skills in a CMV equipped with a machine or equipment.

7.19 Restriction (B)

B restrictions are extremely common in people who have less-than-adequate visual acuity. When driving a commercial motor vehicle, the driver must wear corrective lenses or spectacles.

7.20 Restriction on P

Only Commercial Learner's Permit holders are eligible to receive a P restriction. It indicates no passengers besides the driving instructor and other approved individuals. All license classes, limitations, and endorsements available in the United States are listed above. To earn your license, we can assist you in preparing for the CDL test or endorsement tests through our popular CDL test preparation courses. Every detail you require to obtain your license quickly and always remain safe afterward is included in this course. It is possible to have restrictions placed on a CDL since the driver passed the driving test in a vehicle that did not have certain pieces of required equipment. It is suggested that you undertake the basic skills or road test while driving the business vehicle you attempt to obtain a commercial driver's license. To obtain a Class A CDL to drive a semi-trailer, you must first pass the fundamental skills and road drivers test in a semi-trailer with a manual transmission, as explained above. The E restriction indicates that you will not be permitted to operate a car equipped with a stick shift or automatic transmission.

Given that most semi-trailers are still equipped with manual transmissions, having this Restriction placed on your license will severely restrict your driving choices and career chances. Having a CDL limitation removed from your license is not complicated but can be time-consuming. Again, I strongly advise you to do it right this time and test with the car you intend to drive after earning your CDL. To have a restriction lifted, you may be required to retake the written test and the basic skills or highway driving tests and pay a charge. Be careful to verify how to eliminate a restriction with your given state, as each state has its own set of regulations. CDL codes are letters on your CDL that indicate which restrictions you are subject to. As I previously stated, the most frequently seen limitation codes were V, K, N, M, O, E, Z, & L.

Conclusion

Compared to driving a non-commercial vehicle, operating a commercial vehicle (CMV) necessitates a higher level of education, experience, abilities, and physical capabilities. An applicant for a Commercial Driving license (CDL) must pass both knowledge and skills tests tailored to these better standards to be granted the license. Additionally, when operating any form of a motor vehicle upon public roadways, CDL holders are taken more seriously than non-licensed drivers. Serious traffic offenses made by a CDL holder might harm their ability to keep their CDL certification active and active. Driving a commercial motorized vehicle entails a great deal of accountability. It necessitates the acquisition of specific abilities and information. Most drivers must obtain a valid driver's license (CDL) from their native authority.

Written tests for the commercial driver's license (CDL) are available at all driver license stations. Locations & hours of operation for driver licensing stations can be found on this page. CDL testing is only available by appointment at all driver licensing stations; you can arrange your CDL knowledge exam through the appointment scheduling system. Once you have obtained your Commercial Learners Permit, you may arrange a meeting for your skills tests using the online appointment system. HAZMAT vehicles are not permitted to be used for CDL skills testing. Commercial driver licenses are necessary for all drivers in North Carolina, whether they are paid or volunteer, who operate vehicles designed or utilized to move persons or property. A driver must have a standard driver's license to operate farm vehicles, leisure vehicles, military hardware, fire and emergency response equipment, or fire and rescue vehicles.

The operation of tank trucks, hauling hazardous chemicals, transporting passengers, driving school buses and academic development buses, and pulling double trailers necessitates the acquisition of a specific endorsement in addition to the commercial driver's license. To be qualified for a professional driving license, you need to have extensive experience behind the wheel of your vehicle. It is necessary to have a learner's permit issued at least 6 months before applying for a commercial driving permit. The federal government is working to improve the driver's education curriculum to provide the commercial driving sector with more qualified drivers.

Made in the USA
Coppell, TX
01 September 2022